GW00786470

THE LITTLEST BOOK OF THE SEASONS

with 12 color illustrations

ars edition

© 1984 ars edition
all rights reserved
illustrations by Carmen Deckers,
Elly Christoffel, Peter Glaser,
Gudrun Keussen, Josef Madlener,
Margarete Schoenermark and
Immaculata Weidinger.
edited by Jonathan Roth
printed in West Germany
ISBN 0-86724-063-6

Beautiful is the year
in its coming and going.
Lucy Larcom

Patience is the key
that opens the treasury
of wished-for things
and unlocks each closed-up way.

Anwar-i-Suheili

Give and take makes good friends.

Scottish proverb

It is not possible to step twice
in the same river.

Heraclitus

All excellent things are as difficult
as they are rare.

Baruch Spinoza

Prosperity makes friends,
adversity proves them.

Publius Syrus

Nothing is built on stone:
all is built on sand,
but we must build
as if the sand were stone.

Jorge Luis Borges

Our life is a book that writes itself.
We are characters in a novel
who don't always understand
what the author wants.

Julien Green

One must do more, think less,
and not watch oneself live.

Nicolas-Sébastien de Chamfort

There is one thing alone
that stands the brunt of life
throughout its course:
a quiet conscience.

Euripides

What a heavenly feeling it is,
to follow one's heart.

  Johann Wolfgang von Goethe

To produce things and to rear them,
To produce, but not take possession
  of them.
This is called profound and secret
  virtue.

                              Lao-tse

Wait for the wisest of all counselors:
Time.

Pericles

A light heart and a thin pair of breeches
go through the world cheerily.

Proverb

If you enjoyed this little book, you
should know that there are another
11 titles available.

THE LITTLEST BOOK –

– OF BIRDS
– FOR THE HEART
– OF LIFE
– FOR YOUR BIRTHDAY
– FOR A NEW MOTHER
– OF KITTENS
– JUST FOR YOU
– FOR MOTHER'S DAY
– OF THE SEASONS
– FOR A FRIEND
– OF JOY
– OF ROVING

A NOTE ON QUALITY

The very best of craftsmanship is necessary
in the production of a book this little.
The folded, back-to-back page binding is
from a technique mastered in the orient.
The entire manufacturing process is proudly
presented with authenticated artwork.